# Dreaming of Success

"How to turn your Dreams of Success into your new Reality"

DREAMING OF SUCCESS: HOW TO TURN YOUR DREAMS INTO YOUR NEW REALITY

Copyright © 2010 by Marc D. Alexander
All Rights Reserved

Library of Congress Cataloging-in-Publication Data

ISBN 978-0-557-33112-3

Published by Lulu Inc.

Without limiting the rights under copyright reserved above, no part of this publication may be reproduced, stored in or introduced into a retrieval system, or transmitted, in any form, or by any means (electronic, mechanical, photocopying, recording, or otherwise), without the prior written permission of the copyright owner and the above publisher of this book.

The scanning, uploading, and distribution of this book via the Internet or via any other means without the permission of the publisher is illegal and punishable by law. Please purchase only authorized electronic editions, and do not participate in or encourage electronic piracy of copyrighted materials. Your support of the author's rights is appreciated.

To my family and close friends:
Thank you for giving when everyone else took
Thank you for caring when no one else cared to look
Thank you for believing when everything was out of reach
Thank you for helping me learn for now I am able to teach

- Marc D. Alexander

# Acknowledgements

There are a lot of people that I have to thank for helping me get to where I am today. To name everyone individually would require another book in itself. There are three very important categories that I place those that helped me in which are: Family, friends and believers.

I have been blessed with the best family in the world; The new family that I am starting with my soul mate, my immediate family that raised me and those in my life that have grown to become a part of my family. Thank you for giving me the best life ever! As a child I never knew how tough life was for us. You all did everything possible to ensure that I had a chance in life. I remember wonderful nights of us chasing each other around the house playing tag. I remember waking up early on a Saturday to watch Bobby's World. I remember cleaning up a mess before mom got home so she would not realize that we broke something again. As I matured from a boy to a man, I gained new family members who kept me going on the path to success. From an Upward Bound mentor who still to this date is right there by my side, to my new family in Flint, MI that took me in with open arms to make sure that I made it to graduation. My family is of different ages and different races. They all are a blessing that I am thankful for every single day.

My close friends are some of the best friends that anyone can ask for. I was always around a bunch of friends in my life. When I got my first car I was around a bunch of friends. When I had my first job I was around a bunch of friends. When I was on top of the world I had a bunch of friends. Yes I had a bunch of friends but it was the close friends that were there when I needed a shoulder to lean on. It was the close friends that were there when it seemed like I was on the bottom of the world. It was the close friends that were always there no matter what and I thank all of you so much for that.

There have been people in my life that I have not had the opportunity to build a close friendship with, but it was their belief that I would go on to do great things that has opened so many doors in my life. Thank you for emailing colleagues about "this young inspirational guy" that you met. Thank you for giving me the chance as a young entrepreneur when others did not. Most importantly, thank you for believing that one day I will change the world as we know it.

Finally, I want to thank my angel, Angela, for coming into my life. I admire your strength, your drive, but more than anything your love for me. There is nothing better than loving someone that you know loves you back!

# CONTENTS

**Preface**

    1

**Introduction**

    3

**Chapter 1:**
    A New Look on Life     7

**Chapter 2:**
    Write Down Your Dreams to Make them a Reality     17

**Chapter 3:**
    Learn From Kids about the Power of Perception     27

**Chapter 4:**
    Plant the Seeds That You Are Given to Grow the Blessings That You Want     35

**Chapter 5:**
    Why "Why" is the Best Question to ask Yourself     41

**Chapter 6:**
    Learn to do More and More with Less and Less     47

**Chapter 7:**
    Be True to Your Word     53

**Chapter 8:**
    Good Credit is not Always a Three Digit Number     59

**Chapter 9:**
    Maintaining Your New Reality     67

**Chapter 10:**
    Sharing the Dream     75

**Success Stories**     81

# PREFACE

Dreaming of Success was designed to be a straight to the point read about what you have to do today to change tomorrow. Sometimes all we need is a word of encouragement or a way to dig deep within ourselves to find those words when it seems like no one else cares to remind us. The steps within this book are small but very powerful ways to achieve anything that you put your mind to. It can be material items you seek, a new career, or a needed change in the way you are living your life. Whatever it may be that you are looking, for this book can help you achieve it.

    I was a dreamer who dreamed about obtaining everything that I put my mind to. I dreamed of having a beautiful family, working for a wonderful company and the great life that many of us seek. At the end of every day I realized it was just that, a dream! It was not until I learned the steps, that you will soon read, that taught me how to make my dreams a reality. It was then I realized that the only thing stopping me from being successful was *me*. I was the only true road block in my life. I found that if I believed that I would achieve minutely, then my success was indeed at a minimum. Once I started believing in myself, the dreams that I remembered day after day became reality.

    Everything that you want in life starts with you. You are the person who owns the dream so you are the person who controls it. If you want your dreams to become your reality then stay focused on achieving your dreams, take excellent notes, and most importantly enjoy the book.

# INTRODUCTION

It is easy for someone to tell you that you can be anything that you want to be in life. It is easy to believe you can do anything you put your mind to when your family has the finances to support your dreams or when you have well-known associates that can open doors for you that may take years for you to open yourself. It is so easy, when life is easy, to shoot for the moon and land on the stars, but what about those people who never leave the ground?

I believe that it is good to share your success stories with people to be inspiring, but it is more imperative to share the struggles to first move them! A lot of people are not aware of the challenges that I had to endure to get to where I am in life. I am not talking about studying hard to make the All A's honor roll or picking up a part-time job to save up for a new car. Instead, I am talking about becoming a man while I was still a child because of the fear that my mother might die and getting a job so that my home could actually have a household income. These are the circumstances that sometimes prevent us from leaving the ground, but I will show you that even with the world against you that you can still accomplish anything.

For the longest, people used to think that I lived in a large house in some gated community. When I would bring friends home from school, they would glance around my neighborhood wondering if I somehow made a wrong turn. We got closer to the where my apartment was located they saw the run down homes and the group of people shooting dice at the park as. See, I wasn't born with a silver spoon in my mouth; I was born with one of those plastic sporks. I have experienced the wonderful ups and the devastating downs in my life, but each of those experiences has helped me get where I am today.

What helped me steer myself down the path to success was simply taking the time to think about my actions. I will not sit here and tell you that I never made a bad decision, but I made sure that I at least thought about my decisions beforehand. In life you have those who need to put their hands in fire to understand that it is hot and you have those who watch others put their hand in the fire and learned that it was hot. Well, I was the person that watched. Watching was how I was able to avoid some of the challenges of peer pressure that many youth face. I've been approached to sell drugs, steal, rob stores and the list just goes on and on, but I watched the consequences of these crimes and I knew that wasn't the route I wanted to take.

I did not get where I am because it was handed to me, I got where I am because I went after it. I did not put limits on how far I could go in life and removing those limits allowed me to dream without any boundaries. I could have ran with some of the local dealers or dropped out and quit school but I did not want to limit my dreams to the dreams of some of my peers. I wanted more in life and going down those paths would not have gotten me there.

I realized that I could be anything I wanted just as long as I put in the work to do so. I didn't let society dictate what I was capable of and would become in life. I did not let someone who has never walked in my shoes determine how far I would walk in life. I was not trying to impress my peers, but instead impress the man in the mirror. Every morning that I wake up, he is the person I evaluate as I gaze in the mirror. For me to begin living my dream, all I had to do was decide that I wanted better in life.

# Dreaming of Success

# CHAPTER ONE

## A NEW LOOK ON LIFE

The world ends where the mind stops thinking. When you stop thinking about what could be and settle for what is, everything around you does just that, settle. The dreams of living a prosperous life disappear and the perceived reality of being content sets in. Your most powerful weapon shuts off and your limited reality sets in. We are all put into different situations, with different obstacles placed before us in life. Some of us are born into extremely wealthy families and some of us are born into extremely poor families. We just have to remember that no matter our past or current situations we can always change our future outcomes. This is what I had to learn to do before I would experience true success.

Like many, I was not born into a financially wealthy family. In fact, I was born and raised in a small one bedroom apartment in good ole Pontiac, MI with a mother who had very little finances but an amount of love that money could never buy. I did not have much but I could not let that stop me from trying. What often happens is that we allow our tough situations to overshadow our dreams of escaping that situation. We focus so much on how hard it is to get out of the situation that we lose focus on how we can actually get out of it. My situations kept me dreaming. Dreaming of one day owning my own business, living comfortably, driving my luxury car down a beautiful road with the windows rolled down and the sun shining in my face. It was that dream that kept me going through my darkest hours. It was the "what if" factor that made my dreams become reality. What if I would have never given up, would I have been that millionaire? What if I pushed harder, could that winner had been me? What if I did not give up yesterday, would my blessing have come today? What if the world you dream of could be your reality tomorrow? What if the items you sought out could be possessions you hold tomorrow? It was the "what if" that helped me look at life different and to help you do the same I will show you how!

> *"The World Ends Where the Mind Stops Thinking"*

The first thing that you have to do is stop looking at your obstacles as obstacles and see them as opportunities. You can always create a positive perspective from a negative experience, but you have to be willing and able to change the way you view the experience. For years I viewed not having my father in my life as a challenge. As a child I would ask my mother "Why doesn't my dad want me?" She would reply "Because I love you so much that I wanted you all to myself" as a way to help me hold back my tears. As a teen I would get upset when my friends' fathers would participate in activities that I wished my father and I could take part in. I did everything I thought a good son would learn from a father. I went to church, I helped others and even volunteered in my community yet, I was not given the joy of catching a football thrown from my father or having the man talks that each son desires with his father. The absence of my father made me full of emotions. I was sad because I felt, as nice as I was, that I deserved to have him in my life. I was angry because there were days when I needed him in my life. Most of all I was confused because I could not figure out why I did not have him in my life. I would go 22 years without ever knowing who he ever was but it wasn't until I viewed my obstacle as an opportunity that I would finally meet him.

As I laid in bed one night asking myself how would I feel if I ever met him it dawned on me that his absence was the best presence that I had growing up. I was so determined not to be like him that I did not see how much of a man I had become at such a young age. I was so determined to provide for my family in the future that I took the time to learn the skills necessary to be successful. I was so determined to be involved in my family's life that I took the time to be with and grow with them. I was so determined to be nothing like him that I became everything that I wanted to be. That was the first time that I smiled as I wondered what it would be like to meet my father. I saw the opportunity instead of the obstacle for not having him in my life and was able to now appreciate that opportunity. I was able to move past what I considered to be an obstacle and now have the opportunity to have my father in my life.

I let the negatives overshadow the positives and was not able to see the opportunity until I changed how I viewed the situation. This is just one situation where I was able to create a new look on life. Your situation may be different, but you have to sit back and reevaluate the situation to see the opportunity. This is what you must do in order to move closer to success. This is your first step in changing your future to obtain the life of success you seek.

While at school a good friend and professor of mine pulled me aside and acknowledged my drive and ambition. As we walked through the campus halls, he began explaining the disparity he had noticed in the students. The students who had some of the finer things in life took their schooling for granted. I am not talking about having big houses or fancy cars, but the ability to go to school, eat three meals a day or access a library to help further their education. The students who grew up with very few resources took advantage of every opportunity presented to them that the other students may have passed up. He began recalling various times when the students lacking in resources would come in hours early to do lab work and would sometimes stay all night to complete the work. The other students would only allocate small amounts of time in the lab and sometimes did not show up. They lacked the appetite for success, which in the long run may cause them to miss out on some wonderful opportunities. It was then that I realized how lacking in resources can be a positive in various situations.

My sister and I sat at the table one night anxious for our mom to bring dinner to the table. There were place settings for three but my mom only brought out two plates. "Where is your plate mom?" I asked as she handed us our plates. "I'm not hungry" she replied. My sister and I were too young to understand at the time but we did not have enough food for my mom to eat dinner with us that night. For years I pondered about the secret meals my mom had eaten that always had her full at dinner time. When I later learned that the secret meals were actually missed meals I felt devastated. I had a mental image of my sister and I at the dinner table happily eating and my mom in the kitchen sadden by our financial situation.

That image of us struggling turned into my drive for us to succeed. I wanted to make sure that anytime we cooked as a family that we ate as a family. It was tough growing up in poverty, but when discouraging challenges were in my path to success, I just remembered how bad I wanted to change our situation. I remembered how hard it was growing up. I remember how with a pocket full of pennies and hearts full of love we made it through. Success was the only thing that could satisfy my hunger and I would endure any obstacle to satisfy that hunger. When an opportunity presented itself I jumped on it immediately. There were days where I grew tired of pushing forward but when you want a better life for yourself you will manage to find the strength necessary to keep moving. My strength was my childhood of limited resources. My poverty filled past went from a challenging memory to a positive inspiration to achieve more.

# ACTIVITY ONE

## A NEW LOOK ON LIFE

Let's work on looking at your current obstacles as opportunities. The idea is to highlight the opportunities within your current obstacles. Here are some of the obstacles that I reevaluated to notice the opportunity within.

## OBSTACLE

Not being able to afford to take classes during my last year of college.

Not having my father in my life.

## OPPORTUNITY

Seeing my peers graduate made me value my education more now than I did prior to the obstacle

My drive to be a better man than him allowed me to become the positive man I am today.

## OBSTACLE

_____

_____

_____

_____

_____

_____

## OPPORTUNITY

_____

_____

_____

_____

_____

_____

## OBSTACLE

_____
_____
_____
_____
_____
_____

## OPPORTUNITY

_____
_____
_____
_____
_____
_____

## OBSTACLE

_____
_____
_____
_____
_____
_____

## OPPORTUNITY

_____
_____
_____
_____
_____
_____

# CHAPTER TWO

## WRITE DOWN YOUR DREAMS TO MAKE THEM A REALITY

> "The difference between a dream and a goal is a plan"
>
> - Paul R. Kovatch

A dream is only a dream if we never write it down. When we write down our dreams it allows us to put into perspective what is needed to accomplish those dreams. Do this for any dream you seek to accomplish. If you dream of being a world renowned doctor, write it down. If you dream of being a well known actor, write it down. If you dream of being the first person to live on the moon, write it down. When you write down your dreams you can determine what actions must be taken to achieve them.

While in college I decided that I was going to be a millionaire. Every year I would say "This year I am going to be a millionaire." And at the end of each year I would say "Next year I am going to be a millionaire." Because I did not write it down I could not put into perspective what I had to do to become a millionaire, all I knew is that I wanted to become one. What I did one night in my dorm room would help me become a millionaire. I wrote down that "I will be a millionaire by 25." That's right, with just five dollars in my pocket I made a stand that night that I would be a millionaire by 25. Now that I had it written down I began to understand what it was going to take to become a millionaire by 25. I knew that the road would not be easy but I could focus on my goals now that I wrote them down.

I taped little pieces of paper all over my dorm room to remind myself everyday that I would be a millionaire by 25. I put one over my closet mirror so that every time I got dressed I would remember that today I was dressing to become a millionaire. I would put one on my desk wall to remind me while studying that I was learning to become a millionaire. I also put one on the back of my dorm room door so that before I left to take on the world, I knew that I was fighting to be a millionaire by 25. I had over a dozen pieces of paper that read "I will be a millionaire by 25" in my room. I put one in a very important place that helped on those days that seemed like that dream was out of reach. When I would come back to my dorm room, beat down from the challenges I endured that day I would stare at the ceiling ready to give up until I would read the paper had I taped to the ceiling for just such an occasion that read "I will be a millionaire by 25."Placing those notes all around the room reminded me that the road would be tough but the dream was still within reach. They reminded me of the actions that I needed to take and of the skills that I needed to learn to be a millionaire by 25.

Now I want you to write down 10 things that you dream of obtaining or becoming. They could be career goals, short goals or personal goals. Whatever it may be that you dream of, write it down. Keep a copy on you and at home. When you are on the go and have some time to sit down pull out that piece of paper and remind yourself that everything you do today should be moving you towards making those dreams a reality. When you get home for the day grab that list of dreams and as you reflect on the day ask yourself "Did I do what was needed to make my dreams a reality?" If you were not successful that day do not panic, because you still have tomorrow to complete what you were not able to accomplish today. That is the good thing about dreams, they do not disappear because of a bad day, they remain there as motivation to make the next day better.

There have been many days when I felt that I did not fulfill what was needed to acquire my dreams, but it was knowing that tomorrow was another day to achieve them that kept me going. I had awaken one morning with success on my mind. I was ready to take on any hurdle put before me that day. I had just recently completed one year of successfully being in business for a non-profit organization that I started while in college called Youth of Tomorrow. We completed our first full year of business with a beautiful banquet for the participants in our Engineers of Tomorrow program. I felt great. I was set to meet with an individual that a friend of mine thought would be a good contact to talk with. He told me that the gentleman was running a non-profit as well and could probably give me some pointers for continued success with Youth of Tomorrow. He did not know the guy personally but said it couldn't hurt to talk with him. I received the email informing me to stop by to talk and I was on my way. As I walked into the building I just thought about how I was going to use the information to grow the business and how I could do programming in multiple cities. I was excited.

As I walked in he said "Grab a seat. I've heard a lot about you. What can I do for you?" Excited I began to tell him about Youth of Tomorrow and how I planned on making it a nationally recognized organization. He smiled and I thought to myself here comes the good news. "That sounds good but it will not last. You are too young and should focus on finishing school instead of growing this non-profit." He went on to say more, but I zoned out from the hurt of being told that my dream was impossible. My good mood vanished in an instant and I was now mentally drained as I listened to what seemed like the worst conversation ever. He finished by saying "You should come work with my non-profit if you are so interested in helping youth. I plan on opening a school for challenged youth to attend within the coming years." As I walked out of the office, carrying the now shattered confidence, I began to doubt myself. I began to say "Maybe I should stop and just focus on school. Maybe I should consider working for him."

It would be a long journey back to the dorm room that day. I closed the closest door with the taped paper on it. Walked past the desk where I had taped another piece of paper and fell face first into my pillow. I was drained and that energetic young man that woke up that morning had vanished. How could he tell me that my dream was not obtainable? I worked hard every day to make that dream a reality and he said without hesitation that it was not possible. We all have days like these; where one word can crush our spirits and discourage us from moving on. The dream-buster deflates our dreams making it seem as if our dreams are out of reach. We then settle for the reality that they have created for us and forget the dream that we already had in place. It was not until I rolled over and saw my paper that I had taped on my ceiling that I remembered *my* dream. I remembered that it was *my* dream and not his. I was the one who wanted to be a millionaire by 25 and not him. I began to smile. I began to dream again!

These "dream-busters" can be peers, friends, and even family members. Sometimes they do not mean to intentionally cause harm but they may respond in a way that seems harmful because they cannot comprehend the dream that you have. You have to be careful who you share your dreams with because everyone will not see the world as you do. Robert Kiyosaki (2002) mentioned in Retire Young Retire Rich that "What you think is real is your reality." You have to be able to expand your reality to make your dreams real. Not everyone is able to expand their reality therefore when you share your dreams with other individuals, their inability to dream big may negatively impact you when you share your new reality with them thus, they become "dream-busters."

I always had aspirations of being a very successful business owner. I began reading business books, learning about business plans and eventually incorporated my first business, Youth of Tomorrow, in 2006. I was 21 with my first business and felt great. I expressed this same great feeling to my family and friends. Some loved the idea and some did not. "You should just focus on school and get a job" someone told me. "The resources aren't there and you will have a better chance at getting a job with your degree. I heard how tough it can be with running your own business and maybe you should just wait until you get your life together." To them, they were just concerned for my well-being and thought getting a job was the more secure option compared to entrepreneurship. It frustrated me at first to hear those responses, but I had to realize that some people are only aware of being the employee and not the employer. This is their reality and they are only sharing with you what they believe to be true. I was able to put into perspective what it was going to take to become successful and I was ready to do whatever it took to get there.

> *"What you think is real is your reality"*
> *- Robert Kiyosaki*

I am not telling you to start a business tomorrow and you will be successful. Whatever your dream is it takes time, planning and commitment, but the potential to reach your dream is always there with anything that you dream. There will be days that you want to give up, but you cannot let the forces around you affect the dream within.

> *"If you're walking down the right path and you're willing to keep walking, eventually you'll make progress"*
> *- Barack Obama*

When we do not write down our dreams we lose focus of what we must do to obtain them. I received a call one day from a concerned parent who wanted me to talk to her grandson about his unruly behavior. I had previously spoken with him prior to this occasion, but it seemed that he had forgotten the dream that we discussed. I asked him what it was that he had written down the last time we spoke. He said "I wrote down that I wanted to be a football player, a FBI agent or go to the Navy." I then asked him how has his recent actions put him closer towards those dream and he was taken aback. After a minute of silence he replied "It hasn't. I stopped reading my dreams and began listening to my friends." His friends saw his dream as impossible and he discarded the list because he allowed the "dream-busters" to impact his reality. Once he discarded the list, the dreams began to slip away and the reality of his friends began to set in.

Dreams can be powerful, but easy to forget if you do not remind yourself of them. Writing them down not only serves as a reminder, but as a road map to make the dream a reality. Just because you believe in the dream does not mean that everyone else will. My dreams may be different from yours and your dreams may be different from mine but that does not make them any less important. Reality varies from person to person, but reality is what that person believes to be true.

# ACTIVITY TWO

## WRITE DOWN YOUR DREAMS TO MAKE THEM A REALITY

This is the most important step in changing your dreams into your new reality. Write down what it is that you dream of accomplishing so that you can begin to focus on what it is going to take to obtain this new reality. Start by keeping a copy of this list at home and one on you as you travel. This way you will never lose focus of obtaining these dreams.

On the list below, write down the dreams that you have written on your list and put a date indicating when you started the list. You do not have to fill up all the lines if your dreams do not require them. As you accomplish each dream, check it off. Once you have completed your dreams put the date of completion. This is your proof as you go on to teach others how to turn their dreams into their new reality.

| DREAM | START DATE | ASSIGNED DUE DATE | DATE OF COMPLETION |
|---|---|---|---|
| 1. | | | |
| 2. | | | |
| 3. | | | |
| 4. | | | |
| 5. | | | |
| 6. | | | |

# CHAPTER THREE

LEARN FROM KIDS THE POWER OF PERCEPTION

Kids can sometimes be the best dreamers we know because unlike adults, they have not been taught that something is impossible or unattainable. They see a bird flying and try to fly themselves. They watch a movie of a superhero then change their bedroom into a scene from that movie and they become that superhero. Children can easily change their reality and what they envision becomes their new reality.

As I was talking with a good friend of mine, he began to tell me a story about a time that he had taken his grandson to a magic show. On their ride home he recalled how the magician had made a rabbit disappear. My friend told his grandson that the disappearance of the rabbit was an illusion and it really did not disappear. Not thinking much of it he began to explain how the illusion happened, but was startled by the teary eyed grandson. The grandson said in a cracking voice "But it was true, I saw it with my own eyes. I was right there granddad and I saw it." My friend said how he stopped trying to explain how the illusion was done and allowed his grandson to believe that the rabbit had really disappeared. His grandson believed so much in his reality that he was torn when he was told that his reality was not real.

> *What they envision becomes their new reality*

I understood more than ever how powerful perception can be in the hands of someone who desired to change his or her reality. Not only does that individual believe in their new reality, but so do the people that they come in contact with. The following diagram illustrates how perception combined with reality works. We tell ourselves that our dream is reality so much to the point where we believe it is. We believe in it so much that others began to believe in it as well. From there you move beyond believing in the dream to now making it a reality and the dreaming cycle starts over.

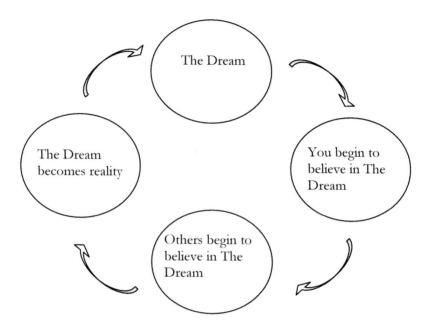

Even in the earliest days of his career Muhammad Ali said that he was the greatest boxer. With every passing match he continued to say that he was the greatest boxer and others also began to believe that he was the greatest boxer. He walked, talked and acted like he was the greatest boxer ever. This dream would soon become reality in Ali's boxing career as he moved up the boxing ranks, and captured the championship title.

The more I began to believe in myself, the more I wanted to change the way the world viewed me as well. With my millionaire dream written down I decided to walk, talk and act like a millionaire. I traded in my baseball cap for ties and turned in my beloved athletic jerseys for suits. I said to myself "If I want to be a millionaire then I need to look like a millionaire." Whenever my classmates and I saw alumni come back to campus dressed in nice suits and ties we would say "I know he is a rich."

> *"Our intention creates our reality"*
> - Wayne Dyer

We knew nothing about the alumnus yet we assumed that they were extremely wealthy. How many times have you saw someone in a nice car or nice outfit that you have never met before and said to yourself "Wow, they look like they are doing great things." The way they carried themselves gave off that image and allowed others to believe in their perceived reality.

You may ask what does other people's belief in my dream have to do with me obtaining it? Well there is a famous saying that "If it walks like a duck, quacks like a duck and looks like a duck then it must be a duck." Believe it or not, but this is how people still perceive one another. If you walk like, look like, and act like your perceived reality then it must be true. When you do this you attract other ducks or in my case millionaires.

One of my biggest breaks came when I decided to look like, walk like and act like a millionaire. I had just received my business cards for an upcoming meeting. I was meeting up with an individual who saw some of my past successes and wanted to talk more over lunch. Unaware at the time, he had decided to bring his business partner along with him. I had on my professional business attire with business cards in hand ready to pass out. After we ate I pulled out my credit card and said "The meal is on me." They were surprised. Being established millionaires for some time now, it was rare that others offered to pay for something for them. Who knew that a lunch meeting would turn into a new business deal? They were impressed after the meeting and decided to invite me to join their circle of business partners. I was no longer walking, talking and acting like a millionaire, I was now becoming one.

# ACTIVITY THREE

## LEARN FROM KIDS THE POWER OF PERCEPTION

In this chapter we talked about how people may perceive an individual based on appearances. So now it is time to impact how people will perceive you!

   I wanted to be a millionaire, so I had to understand how a millionaire looked, talked, and walked. By learning how they talked I was able to understand what they were involved in that allowed them to continue to be millionaires, such as stocks, commodities, businesses and other investments. By understanding how they walked, I now was able to comprehend the skills that I needed to capitalize as a millionaire, such as on the spot business pitches, dining etiquette skills and how to navigate through a room of high net worth individuals to obtain vital information that would keep me a millionaire. I observed how a millionaire looked and was better prepared to positively represent my business no matter where I was. My attire was well presented in both my professional and personal life.

   Not that you've written down your dreams, write down how someone who has already accomplished those dreams would be perceived. So in my case I watched how millionaires walked, talked and looked then modified the way people perceived me to reflect that of a millionaire.

When I see a (n)_____, they are _____
_____

How are _____ perceived? They are perceived as
_____
_____
_____

# CHAPTER FOUR

## PLANT THE SEEDS THAT YOU ARE GIVEN TO GROW THE BLESSINGS THAT YOU WANT

Now that you believe in yourself and others believe in you, it is now time for you take advantage of opportunities for your new reality. This is where it can get tricky. Most of the time, we are seeking opportunities when it is unnecessary to do so. Sometimes, opportunities are right there in front of us waiting to be utilized. When evaluating an opportunity, do not just look at short-term success, look at the possible growth potential in the long-term as well.

I can recall sitting in church one Sunday morning as the pastor said "When you ask God for blessings he gives you seeds." I found his words intriguing! He went on to say "If you ask for money, he will give you a job. If you ask for a garden he will give you the seeds to plant and grow your garden." The message in itself was very powerful. When you are attempting to make your dream a reality you have to evaluate the tools that you are given to accomplish this goal. For me, I wanted to be a millionaire by 25 and after leaving church that day I realized that my seeds to making my dream a reality were the businesses that I owned. They were in front of me the whole time, yet I overlooked their true potential. Separately they contributed a nice amount of revenue to help me become a millionaire by 25. By leveraging the potential of all of them combined, my dream became a reality now more than ever.

I was now able to see a better way to acquire my dream. Instead of climbing the tall wall, I would simply walk around it. I was now watering my seeds to grow my goal. As simple as walking around the wall may seem, even to the smartest person it is sometimes extremely hard to do. We become so centered on climbing to the top that we get tunnel vision. We do not see anything else except the top of the wall. The sides begin to vanish and a bright light shines at the top and that is all we see. This is how we sometimes overlook our seeds when seeking our dreams. It may be noticeable by others, but it still takes us a while to see it.

We have all either experienced it ourselves or seen others who have done this. I had a childhood friend whose father was a wealthy individual. While driving one day he says to me "I want to be a millionaire." I thought to myself that should be easy seeing how your dad is already a millionaire. Quiet for a minute he shouted "Marc I want you to sit down with me and tell me what you think of my business idea." After a few meetings he went forward with his first business idea. A few months later he came back and said "I have another idea I want you to look at. The other one did not work, but I know that this one will." We sat down again and came up with a game plan for his new idea and again he came back after he encountered some obstacles seeking a new venture to create. During this entire process he did not seek the advice of his father. He was so focused on becoming his own millionaire that he never thought about asking his millionaire dad how he became one. He wanted to climb the wall instead of walking around it. His tunnel vision prevented him from seeing the seed that was already in front of him.

What seeds have you recently overlooked? Have you neglected to read a book that someone recommended you read or have you procrastinated completing that task you were suppose to finish last week?

# ACTIVITY FOUR

## PLANT THE SEEDS THAT YOU ARE GIVEN TO GROW THE BLESSINGS THAT YOU WANT

Sometimes we seek blessings without knowing that they have been with us all along. I had to sit down and look at everything in my life to see that the resources I needed to become a millionaire were right there. I was so focused on making a million dollars with one business that I overlooked the capital potential when I combined all of my resources together. Write down what it may be that you are seeking to accomplish your dreams. Once written down thoroughly look at all of the current resources that you have and analyze the strengths of your resources and how, with those combined strengths, you can leverage them to get closer to your dreams.

# CHAPTER FIVE

## WHY "*WHY*" IS THE BEST QUESTION TO ASK YOURSELF

As a child my mother would sit me at the dining room table and ask me a series of why questions. I would reach for a crayon to color with and she would ask "Marc, why are you reaching for that crayon?" I would pause, tightly closing my eyes to ponder why then reply "Because I want to color." As I began to color she would ask "Why did you pick that color crayon to color with?" I would pause again and reply "Because this is my favorite color to color with." It was these *why* questions at a young age that would keep me asking *"why"* and "what if" as I went through life. *Why* became a powerful question in both challenging and advantageous situations.

It had been a long month. That's right, a month. A month of obstacle after obstacle after grueling obstacle. I was simply beat and ready to throw in the towel. Business was slow, school was hard and it seemed like the world around me was crumbling. Everywhere I turned, there seemed to be nothing but bad news. "That's it! I'm done!" I said as I headed for the bathroom to take what seemed like a two hour shower. During that time I reflected on the day and began to ask myself why everything turned out the way it did, and what I should do about it. As I leaned my head against the shower wall I began to reflect on those days when my mom would ask me *why* a million times. I thought about how I would think so hard for an answer only to be asked *why* again. But today was different. As I thought about being asked *why* over and over and over again, I realized that when she could no longer ask me *why* that I had gotten to the real answer. The truth was that "I was tired because I did not get any sleep after staying up all night watching movies" answer. I must have asked myself why a hundred times in the shower until I got to the real answer. After a hundred whys it was only one why left.

"Why can't I give up right now and just throw in the towel?" That was the *"why"* that made me think the most. It made me think of the many reasons why I couldn't quit. My reasons *"why"* were so powerful that I said I would never give up no matter what. I was tired of struggling just to get by another day to only struggle even more. I came too far to turn back and go down the road that I was trying to get off of. I did not know if tomorrow would be the day for my dreams to become a reality and giving up now would never help that dream come true. My *why* was so powerful that I did not dwell on the how to get rich but instead the "*why*" I wanted to become rich. The *why* made finding "how" easy, because I was so driven to accomplish it.

Let's start by looking back at something that was not accomplished or that you gave up on. Now ask yourself why you did not accomplish that particular task or assignment. After you have developed an answer, ask yourself why again. Continue to do this until you can no longer ask yourself why. This exercise allows you to get the root cause of the problem a majority of the time. When you find the real why, you can develop a more accurate solution to the situation.

# ACTIVITY FIVE

## WHY "WHY" IS THE BEST QUESTION TO ASK YOURSELF

In order to solve a problem you have to get to the root of the problem. If you do not get to the root cause of the problem it will not disappear, but instead lay dormant until it becomes a problem again. So for this activity we will get to the root of some of your challenges.

First you will need to write down your challenges. After writing them down ask yourself "Why" did this happen. After answering the question rewrite your answer on the next line and ask yourself "Why" again. Repeat this until you get to the root cause of the problem. Here is my example.

1. Did not get a good grade on my Calculus II test.
   **"WHY"**
   Because I didn't study

2. I didn't study
   **"WHY"**
   Because I was tired over the weekend

3. I was tired over the weekend
   **"WHY"**
   Because I was playing videogames all day

4. I was playing videogames all day
   **"WHY"**
   Because I enjoy them so much that I procrastinate

To fix the problem I would only play the game either during a vacation or once I have completed all of my work to avoid getting another bad test score.

# CHAPTER SIX

LEARN TO DO MORE AND MORE
WITH LESS AND LESS

People sometimes look at hitting rock bottom as the worse experience ever but it is when you hit rock bottom and *stay* there that it becomes the worst experience ever. Usually when you reach rock bottom you become most dangerous. You have little resources, very little time, but you still have so much to do. You now have to be innovative and find a way to keep up with your responsibilities with less resources then you had to start with. Someone once told me that dawn comes after the darkest hour. When it seems like the world is against you and nothing looks like it is working for you **Do Not give up**. This is where most people give up and lose the dream. This is where everything that you have learned up to this point helps you transition that dream into your new reality.

Life was great. It seemed like I had everything as I wheeled around in my office chair. I got up, walked past the kitchen through the lobby and out the front door expecting today to be just like every other day. I met up with some of my business partners as we planned for a big profitable event. I was ready for everything except for the calls that seemed to all come in simultaneously with bad news. It would have been great if it was just for one company, but each company that I owned seemed to all have bad news. I fell straight from the top of the world down to the depths of earth. I was now juggling all of my problems at once at a time that seemed like the fall of my success.

> *... when you hit rock bottom and stay there that it becomes the worst experience ever*

Recall earlier how I said you have to be able to look at every situation as an opportunity and how that opportunity may be the seed that you had always been looking for? Well this was one of those opportunities and a seed that helped grow a garden of blessings.

That year I had to do more and more with less and less. I had to cut the fat from my work situation and become a lean machine. That was a tough year for me in business, but still a blessing. It was a blessing because I learned to work with scraps while still competing with those who had full plates. When the economy took a toll, I witnessed a vast amount of large companies go under. My business lost a lot of corporate partners. It was tough to watch large companies that I had worked with vanish over night. Had I not went through those challenging phone calls that day, I may have vanished that day along with the others. I had endured a dark hour and was now able to see daylight again.

The best dinner that I have ever had was a dinner at a restaurant with my mom. It wasn't that the food was great, but I was looking at the reality that we had dreamed of for years. My mom was a single parent, cancer survivor and she had dreams of becoming a nurse. She wrote down two very important dreams that she made a reality. One was that she wanted to graduate from college before my sister and I. The second one was that she wanted to become a LPN. The typical person would have looked at us and said that our dreams were impossible. How could a cancer survivor who had been out of school for years plan to graduate from school within a few short years as a LPN before her two teenage children? People would look at us as if our dreams were some made up fantasy. They were right. Our dreams were a fantasy to them, but they were our dreams. To them it was unimaginable but to us it was a reality.

As I put down my menu I said "Mom.", pausing to take it all in "We did it! Look at us! This is what we said we would do years ago and we did it!" I sat dressed in a nice three piece suit after a long day of meetings with other business executives and she sat dressed in her nursing attire after a long day of work. She was now taking her classes to become a RN and I was now an owner of multiple businesses. We did it. We made our dreams a reality. The long days and hard work were all worth it. I could not have painted a better picture if I had the skills of Michelangelo.

Why did I choose to share this you may ask? I shared this to express how obtaining my dreams was tough but worth every second that I sat there soaking in the dreamed reality. It will be the same feeling for you when you look up and see your dreams become your new reality.

# ACTIVITY SIX

## LEARN TO DO MORE AND MORE WITH LESS AND LESS

In this activity you will learn to unlock the innovative thinker within. When we are put into tough situations, it can sometimes render our thinking abilities. We become so overwhelmed with trying to figure out how to accomplish everything that we shutdown and lose our train of thought.

First, you need to write down everything that needs to be done for you to reach your goals. Here is list of the things that I had to do for my company's program as an example:

1. Pick-up a rental van
2. Come up with the money to pay in advance
3. Drop the van off Friday night at the site
4. Pick the van up Saturday morning to transport program participants
5. Have someone follow me to drop the van off

Instead of getting frustrated and shutting down I wrote my challenges down so that I could evaluate them. What I did was seek out a transportation company to avoid picking up the van. Next, I arranged to pay them after the service was completed, which saved me the time of paying in advance. I then established an agreement where the participants would be picked up and dropped off by the transportation company. After everything was done, I actually spent less money and time than I did when I was juggling all of my problems. By writing them down and developing a solution for each of my problems I was able to accomplish the tasks with fewer resources.

# CHAPTER SEVEN

BE TRUE TO YOUR WORD

Now that you know how to turn your dreams into reality, it is important that you learn how to maintain that reality. Like anything in life, it can go just as fast as it came but one of the most powerful weapons that you have in maintaining this reality is your word. When you tell someone that you are going to do something it then becomes an agreement. Even the smallest agreements have a lasting impact on an individual. This is very important in your professional and personal life. If you can practice keeping your word then keeping up with your dreams will be no problem.

Keeping your word can even affect the dreams that you wrote down. When you keep your word, you can look back and enjoy the new reality knowing that you stayed true to your word, but most importantly yourself. On our quest to obtain our dreams we aspire to be the best that we can be, but when you are not true to the word even your best reality can become painful.

In high school I was a member of the National Geographic Globe Trotters. The group leaders, Mr. and Mrs. Arsen, took time to expose a wonderful group of Pontiac youth to the exciting world of National Geographic. We would meet each month at an upscale restaurant and converse about the National Geographic books that we had received that month. One particular day, we had one of our state representatives in attendance as our keynote speaker. He seemed to be on top of the world. Everything that he set his eyes on he was able to obtain. He began to say how he always wanted to be this well-known politician with a wonderful family. Well he made that a reality. He was now one of the most well-known politicians in the state. It wasn't until I asked an innocent question that brought on a moment of silence by him. "If you could change anything what would it be?" He had a worried look on his face and he said "I wished that I would have spent more time with my kids. Those are years that I can never get back and if I could change anything I would have spent more time with them."

Turning your dreams into a reality is one of the best feelings ever. Seeing everything you thought about within arms reach is breathtaking, but it can be the small promise that we made to ourselves that we sometimes forget when our dreams become our reality. I will spend more time with my family when I become successful. I will donate to charity when I get wealthy. I will make it to church every Sunday when I get my car. Always remember that small things in life count too. Do not be the person that looks back on their life and realize that their new reality only harmed the realities of their loved ones. I cannot say how that politician felt that day, but his face said enough for me to know that he was hurt. Keep your dreams a reality by first keeping your word.

# ACTIVITY SEVEN

## BE TRUE TO YOUR WORD

For this activity we will utilize a small note book or sticky notes. Anytime you agree to do something write it down in your notebook or on sticky notes. Put deadlines by each task that you have written down. Be sure to set the deadlines earlier than their expected due date. For instance, I needed to make reservations for an event and registration ended Friday. I wrote down the task and set my deadline for Wednesday. This way if I was too busy to do it Wednesday I still had a time cushion to get it done. I made registrations Thursday and completed my task as I had written down.

# CHAPTER 8

## GOOD CREDIT IS NOT ALWAYS A THREE DIGIT NUMBER

As your dreams become a reality keep in mind that people are watching. Seeing you go from a dream world to a new real world would not only amaze yourself, but those who know about you as well. As people began to learn more about me, they became amazed when they saw how far in life I had come. I was leaving rags and on the road to riches.

By now you are probably wondering what my reality is like if I am telling you about making your dreams a reality. Well, the best way to explain my new reality is a Disney Movie jammed packed with all types of unthinkable magic. When you write down your dreams and do what it takes to accomplish them, there is nothing that can prevent you from obtaining that dream and one of my dreams was to finish college.

An obstacle that was put before me was paying for school. I had just one year left and not enough money to pay for it. I was someone who had climbed the ranks fast and was now at a road block that seemed impossible to get around. This was one of the results of that dreadful day of bad news phone calls. Everything from my professional to my personal life was affected. I had to come up with $16,000 in one week if I wanted to get back into school and could not get approved for a single loan. Frustrated by my financial burden, I still decided to push on and chased after my dreams. One day I received a phone call from a reporter who had previously written several news stories about me and my service to the community. She asked how were some of the students paying for school in these tough economic times. I told her that I had no idea because I was not able to pay for school either. She paused and then replied "But you are Kettering University's Star Senior." Staying positive, I told her that everyone was feeling the tough times and that the money just wasn't there. We talked a little longer then it was back to chasing the dreams for me.

A few days had passed and I was up again ready to change my reality not knowing that it was already changing for me. I received a phone call from a good friend who said, as soon as I answered the phone, "Great article in today's paper. You are a great person and I know something good will happen for you." Curious about the comment I grabbed a copy of the paper and there it was on the front page "Marc Alexander already has racked up more than $130,000 in debt to attend Kettering University and he has 12 classes still to go." The article was beautiful, but it wasn't until a few days later that the magic began to happen.

While visiting my grandmother I received another phone call. I looked at the phone and it was my school calling. I was debating on answering the phone assuming that it was a reminder about the bill that I had racked up. I took a deep breath and said "Hello" ready to hear the bad news. Excited she replied "I have some very good news for you." Shocked by the response I began to wonder what had her so happy and what good news did she have. "I have a letter here for you and attached to the letter is a check for $16,000 with your name on it." That would be the first night that I was anxious to wake up and go to the financial aid office.

I woke up an hour before the alarm clock and took off for the financial aid office. As I entered the campus center I began to glow and everyone could see it. I darted up the campus stairs, too excited to wait for the elevators which for some reason goes to the 5th floor before it does the main floor. I walked into the office and read the letter that showed me that any dream can come true. It read:

*Dear Mr. Alexander,*

*Enclosed is a cashier's check for $16,000. This is a gift to pay for your classes next term at Kettering. We hope that at some time in your successful future you may find someone in need and "pay this gift forward."*

*Sincerely,*

*Flint friends who are grateful for Kettering University and its outstanding graduates.*

"Pay it forward." That was all that they asked. An anonymous check for $16,000 with a request that I just pay it forward.

Understand that when you decide to turn your dreams into a reality that the only thing that can stop you is you. Had I given up on my dreams there is no telling where I would be today. Now, at the age of 24 I have a beautiful fiancé, a bachelor degree from one of the top engineering schools in the country and the opportunity to obtain absolutely anything that I want in life. My dreams are now my reality and I am enjoying every second of it. So what reality are you dreaming of?

# ACTIVITY EIGHT

## GOOD CREDIT IS NOT ALWAYS A THREE DIGIT NUMBER

Now that you have completed the previous activities, this activity will serve as your personal credit report. Go back and look over everything that you have done and evaluate how you are doing in completing the activities needed to accomplish your dreams. Do this every few weeks to ensure that you do not stray from the new reality that you will soon acquire.

# CHAPTER NINE

## MAINTAINING YOUR NEW REALITY

Once you have accomplished turning your dreams into your reality, you have to be prepared to maintain that reality. This is an important step that is often neglected once we accomplish a major goal. You will need to put the same amount of effort into maintaining the reality as you did attaining it.

What usually happens after we have accomplished the dream is that we get comfortable. It is nothing wrong with enjoying the moment, but you have to understand that the accomplishments can disappear if you do not continue to put forth the same effort you applied towards getting them.

Life was great! After successfully launching my third business I began to get comfortable. I said to myself, "Marc. You deserve a break. You have worked hard to get where you are and now it is time to sit back and relax." I purchased the video games that I wanted to play. I went to see all the movies that I missed while working. I was doing absolutely everything except working as hard as I did to accomplish my dream. I was swiping my bank card over and over and over again, until one day I sat down and looked at my bank statement. I was spending more than I was bringing in. I was going right back to where I initially started. It is okay to work hard then play hard later, but I was playing harder than I was working. I had gotten comfortable. I lost focus of what it took to achieve my reality and now it was slipping away.

Let's look at this situation as the purchase of your first new car. You have dreamed of this day when you would be sitting in your first new vehicle. Every weekend you are at the car wash cleaning inside and outside of the car and paying the extra money to get the wax during the wash. You make sure that the oil is changed before the actual due date and you even spend the extra money to hang the car freshener from your rear-view mirror. You tell yourself that you will take care of this car forever. Now, a few months have passed and that new car excitement has wore off. The car washes occur less frequently, the inside of the car is not always vacuumed, and you begin to push the maintenance check-ups back a week. It eventually gets to a point where you have gotten so comfortable with the car that you no longer value it like you did when you first sought it. After awhile, the car is unattractive, needs repairs, and you are back to dreaming about getting a new car again.

Maintaining your new reality is just as important as attaining it. No matter what your dream may be, you are going to have to put in time to continue to live the reality. If you dream of being a successful lawyer, you are going to have to be prepared to take on challenging cases. If you want to be a business owner, you are going to have to make sure that you sustain your business. Whatever your new reality may be, remember the new responsibilities that come with it.

The day that I recognized my new reality was slowly slipping away I understood that the new reality only exists as long as I allowed it to exist. If I decide to stop going to the office and skip out on important meetings then I began to push myself away from the dream that I so anxiously sought out. It is easy for us to blame others for our mishaps, but remember that it was your dreams that inspired you to the change your life, it was your ambition that allowed you to acquire your new reality and it is your fault if your new reality disappears.

"It gets lonely at the top" my friend said as we talked about accomplishing our dreams. "What do you mean by that" I asked. "You have to understand that not everyone aspires for greatness. That's good because it makes it easier to accomplish that success when it is only a selected few that seek it, but in the process you will slowly see yourself grow apart from things you used to do in the past." Smiling I said "I will never change on my path to success. I will do the same thing in the future that I did in the past." I was not aware at the time that this new reality would bring about new responsibilities. He said with a grin "You won't change as an individual, but what you have to do to maintain your new lifestyle will. I had an abundance of friends growing up Marc. I still keep in touch with some of them, but our realities have changed. I can't do what we used to do back in the days because it will not allow me to maintain the new life that I have and sacrificed for for so long. They have become comfortable with their reality whereas I have outgrown it. I wanted better out of life and to keep that better life I had to sacrifice habits from the old one."

Now that I look back on life, I see some of the old habits that I had to sacrifice to maintain my new reality. You do not have to completely give up some of your old habits, but you establish a limit to how often or how much you will do so that it does not negatively impact your life.

Just about every Friday night a lot my friends would go to the clubs in the downtown area. After the clubs let out we would hang around in the parking lot talking with people. After leaving the parking lot we would head to one of the local Coney Island restaurants. After that particular restaurant closed everyone would head over to the next Coney Island. After that restaurant closed everyone would head to one of the local gas stations then eventually part ways. After the night was over we would wake up and do it again. This was like a weekend ritual. It was the same every week yet we continued to do it.

Now that I have obtained my new reality I cannot continue to do what I used to because I want to maintain my reality. I have programs that my company provides to youth on the weekends. I sometimes have meetings and events to go to on the weekends, so I have to sacrifice going out to prepare for these new activities. Yes I enjoyed going out back then with my friends and partaking in the weekend ritual, but I quickly learned when to say no and when to say yes. The weekend ritual would not put me closer to nor help maintain that life-time reality I sought.

> *Maintaining your new reality is just as important as attaining it*

Although I do not participate in the weekend ritual, I still have a tremendous amount of fun with the new activities in my new reality. Instead of all night weekend parties I do evening activities with my wonderful fiancé. We will go out to the movies, travel or just laugh the night away learning new ballroom dances. Instead of indulging in non-stop gaming days, I find times where I stop by my best friend's home and spank him in a game of basketball. I still have fun with my new reality, but it is just at a different capacity then it was back then. I understood that there would be a needed change in my life if this was the new reality that I wanted.

You have to remember during the entire process of attaining and maintaining your new reality that it is just that, *your* reality. You have to take responsibility for your actions because *your* actions will impact *your* reality. Every day that you wake up, you have to value everything that you have accomplished. The moment that you take your accomplishments for granted, they slip away and you have to start the cycle of dreaming that you can attain them over again.

# ACTIVITY NINE

## MAINTAINING YOUR NEW REALITY

Now that you have turned your dreams into your new reality I want you to always value that reality. When you wake up I want you to look around and be thankful for your accomplishments. Be thankful that you have come so far in obtaining this new reality.

If you wake up and you are ready for a new reality then ask yourself what you can do to improve your current reality. Still continue to value that current reality because you put a lot of time into creating it, but begin writing down the new dream and begin changing your reality again.

Use this space to get started.

Now that I am in my new reality, I want to maintain it by: _____
_____
_____
_____
_____
_____
_____
_____
_____
_____

# CHAPTER TEN

## SHARING THE DREAM

My goal in life is to change the world. I will accomplish this goal by implementing change in people through inspirational books and motivational speeches. I want to get personal with my change efforts. I will talk one-on-one with anyone who will listen; with anyone who needs help; with anyone I can inspire! I want everyone everywhere to understand how obtainable anything in life can be. We often get distracted by some of the challenges in today's society and allow them to cloud our judgment. Anything is possible in any situation, but it takes the right tools to forward the action; tools to dream, the tools to take action and the tools to maintain this reality.

You are someone in the process of changing your dreams into your new reality. I need you to tell your family, friends, anyone you meet about the endless possibilities available if they continue to make their dreams a reality. You will have some friends that can read this book then aspire for a better life, but you will have those who need to see it to believe it. You will have those friends who will give up on the dream when the road gets tough. By accomplishing your own dreams you have to be their new life coach to inspire them to not only keep pushing forward, but take that initial step towards accomplishing their dream.

When helping others accomplish their dreams keep in mind that people dream at different levels. Everyone does not dream of being wealthy or obtaining a career. Some people may dream of rebuilding a school or ensuring that less fortunate people have the resources to improve their lives.

I was blessed to be invited to join the Rotary Club of Greater Flint. The Rotary Club is an international service organization that can best be described by the wonderful motto they have of "Service Above Self." I had the opportunity to meet various community leaders, entrepreneurs and passionate members who shared with me their dream, among many others, to eradicate polio. This is a perfect example of how a dream was shared and eventually changed the world. Through their efforts and others such as the Bill & Melinda Gates Foundation, they have been able to inspire people all over the world to support the cause. This all started from a dream, a dream to one day eradicate polio that has now inspired millions to dream as well.

No matter what the dream may be, the impact can still be powerful. Rotary Club was an idea over 100 years ago that has now turned into an organization with 1.2 million members worldwide. If you know someone who dreams of one day changing the world encourage them to believe in and strive for that dream. Show them the tools that you learned in this book to make that dream a reality.

Through the obstacles that I had to endure and overcome in my life, I now understand that anything is possible. Some of the challenges that I had to face seemed absolutely impossible to conquer, but by applying the methods that I have shared you, I was able to come out victorious. Life is what you make it, so how about making it your new reality.

# ACTIVITY TEN

## SHARE THE DREAM

Keep dreaming! Never stop dreaming. Encourage your family, friends and peers to dream big because anything anywhere is possible!

Write a list of family, friends, and peers that you can inspire to keep their dreams alive!

1. _____
2. _____
3. _____
4. _____
5. _____
6. _____
7. _____
8. _____
9. _____
10. _____

# Success Stories

Over the years, I have come across numerous dreamers who have turned those dreams into their new reality. By using the steps in this book you too could become one of these successful dreamers.

During my college years, I was involved in an organization called the Kettering Entrepreneur Society. This was a student ran organization of aspiring entrepreneurs led by our advisor Professor Tavakoli. He informed us as entrepreneurs that we should always be seeking ways to get our businesses to the next level. Once a week we would hold meetings to aid one another in our dreams of being successful business owners. Some of the members had already launched their businesses while in school. Some of these companies were Youth of Tomorrow, Prime Studios LLC, Book Deal Finder and Rate My Student Rental. Although we had started our own businesses, we were all looking for ways to accomplish our dreams of taking those businesses to the top.

One night after a long intense meeting with KES, I remember talking with the owners of Prime Studios LLC, Matt and Brad. "Marc, I know that we are all going to make it" Matt said. "Giving up now is not an option" Brad commented as he walked over to the table. I could see the drive within them. We enjoyed being able to run our own business, but balancing school and our personal lives all at the same time presented a lot of challenges for us. Nights where other students were headed to bed we were headed to meetings. We were planning projects, meeting with clients or evaluating how to modify our businesses to capitalize on the opportunities. On those days when it seemed too tough to push on we served as inspiration to one another to never give up!

February 2010 would turn out to be a very exciting month for us. It was the month where Prime Studios LLC held a grand opening for their new office in Northville. The participants in Youth of Tomorrow's Special Security Agency program were invited to provide security for the event and I was there to bear witness to another dream turned into reality. I began to reflect on the late night KES meeting and the intense discussions for fund request. To see my business helping with their grand opening was priceless. Here were two young entrepreneurs, who like me, dreamed of this day and now it had become their new reality.

Dreamers seeking to change their reality can be some of the most innovative people. What makes them innovative is the tremendous growth that they display as they take on obstacles that most may view as unattainable.

As my career as an entrepreneur began to take-off I started to get a lot of attention from professionals and peers. One person in particular was Donald, the owner of Pryo Blu. Our last year in college, we grew to become great friends and now were professionals. He approached me with some questions about taking on entrepreneurial endeavors. Like many dreamers he had a passion in life. He enjoyed changing the blank canvases of life into works of art. He told me one day as he was showing me some of his work that "This is the best art that you've never seen!" As I viewed the astounding art work I was amazed that someone on campus had the skills and abilities that he possessed. He said "Marc, I know I have the talents to become a very successful artist. I just need to know where to start on my quest to greatness." Happy to help I replied "No problem Don. I would love to help you on your journey." I was thinking about possibly sitting down to go over his plan when he said "How about we talk more over a game of golf." "Sounds great!" I replied as I left the room.

Now this is a perfect example of how dreamers can be innovative. I was a very active person. I played basketball, football and took part in just about any sport that you could think of. Out of every sport that I could play he asked to meet during the one sport I neglected to learn, golf! When I left from talking with him that day, I drove straight to my uncle's house to borrow his PGA videogame and a bag of clubs. I had to learn in one week what others learned in years of training. Needless to say that being the best golfer was not on my dream list, so you can image how my first time at the driving range went.

During our meeting he spoke of doing an upscale art show in Indianapolis. The event would consist of a live band, entrees, champagne and a number of the paintings he created. We began to bounce ideas off one another until we came up with a plan. By securing the right amount of funds and leveraging his resources in Indiana the thought of an art show became more believable now than ever.

We began talking about this art show November 2007 and in April 2008 I found myself riding with some friends down to Indianapolis for Donald's first large scale art show. Everything that he mentioned in the dream was included in the reality. He had a live band, entrees, champagne and a number of the paintings he created. He had taken his skills to new heights and is now designing everything from art to furniture. His dream had become his new reality.

As I mentioned before, dreams do not have to necessarily be material items or career aspirations. For my mother and grandmother their dream was raising a man without a man in his life.

I have to give my mother and grandmother a lot of credit. They did the best job that they could raising me with limited resources. There were many days where all we had were each other and that was it, but I can stand here and say that I had the best childhood ever. It is the time that parents invest in the early years of a child that molds the individuals we see years later.

One day my grandmother received a call from Houston, TX. The first words she heard as she answered the phone were "Mom. I am pregnant and I going to need help raising my son. I do not want my child to grow up without a father." My grandmother replied, "I will be his father! Come home and we will figure out something from there." As time went by she would eventually give birth to a beautiful baby boy. Here was a single parent with a loving mother and now a child.

A friend once told me that when life gives you lemons then make lemonade. Let's just say that growing up we made a lot of lemonade.

When my mom headed to work I headed to my grandmother's for a day of cartoons, candy, but most importantly Toys "R" Us. I would walk through my grandmother's door asking if "we pay check" had came so that we could go explore the isles of Toys "R" Us. Some days I was blessed to be able to get a toy, but others I was just happy to run up and down the store isles until I was too tired to scream "toys." After my mom got off work it was home to see what new adventures I could create as I turned the apartment into my own adventure land.

It wasn't the toys or candy that I enjoyed as a child but the memories that I still to this day treasure with my family. They showed me how to smile, how to play and how to enjoy life. They showed me the power of being polite and how the word "thank you" could take me far in life. I no longer have the toys that we got from Toys "R" Us or the cute clothes that I wore in my school pictures. Instead, I have the images of laughter, the images of fun and the images of my family and I loving one another. These are the memories that, as I continue on my path to success, inspire me to improve the lives of others. These are the memories that encouraged me to dream big as I changed the world around me. It was their dream of changing their reality that allowed me to now change mine.

# ABOUT THE AUTHOR

**Marc Alexander**, a native of Pontiac, Michigan, has never given up on the potential of the city's youth. For the last five years, Marc has taken on the challenge of being a ray of hope for over 300 adolescents in his home town. He could have easily stayed within the enclaves of Kettering University, earned his degree and worked for a Fortune 500 company. Instead, he decided to uplift the students in his community.

When the four community centers that were once beacons of hope for students of Pontiac were closed, thereby eliminating most opportunities for students to participate in recreational sports and afterschool activities, Marc used this opportunity to start his first youth program. In 2005, he purchased four basketball rims for the neighborhood children to play with and orchestrated small basketball tournaments. The summer youth program put on by Marc would lead to the start of his next program, Engineers of Tomorrow, in the fall of 2005, and eventually his first company, Youth of Tomorrow, in June of 2006. Youth of Tomorrow (YofT) is centered around giving kids the opportunity to learn aspects of engineering and other careers that will help them become successful students and that will inspire them to pursue a college degree. YofT's most notable program has been the Engineers of Tomorrow series. For this program, students are transported from Pontiac to Kettering University at least one Saturday a month and given engineering challenges to investigate. As an example, students had to build a robot using very complex engineering understandings like how to read electronic schematics and how to solder components to a circuit board. This program teaches the value of teamwork and persistence, but more than anything it challenges students to use math and science in a practical way. Always looking for ways to improve, Marc has also developed other programs that are designed to inspire the next attorneys and intelligence officers. He has implemented the Special Security Agency program whose most prominent mission was serving as security to the Michigan House of Representative member, Tim Melton, at the State Capitol. In the summer of 2009, Marc partnered with Sky's The Limit Community Foundation to provide recreational basketball for teens. The program was an exact replica of the National Basketball Association (NBA) where students had a draft night, teams had owners and general managers, and the games were set up to have both a regular season and playoffs. Marc also teamed up with the Palace of Auburn Hills to host the championship game for the students in the program. Because of the diligent work Marc put in, students had an engaging and memorable experience and Pontiac has additional resources to support the extra-curricular and educational needs of their students.

Marc has served as an advisor for the Atanga Peace Project which educates and enhances the lives of families in Cameroon, West Africa. He is a business consultant for WOWE 98.9 FM and is on the advisory board for YMCA Camp Phoenix.

Marc earned a bachelor of science in Business Administration from Kettering University, formerly known as General Motors Institute, in December 2009. His accolades include Kettering University Student of the Year 2009, Student Alumni Council Distinguished Leader 2009, and National Society of Black Engineers Member of the Year 2007. He is a four time winner of the Kettering University Innovation Challenge 2008-2009, and U of M Launch Social Entrepreneur Champion of 2009. Marc continues to make an impact on the lives of others through his success as an entrepreneur and his words as a motivational speaker.